Cyrus Morton Cutler

Letters From the Front

From October 1861 to September 1864

Cyrus Morton Cutler

Letters From the Front
From October 1861 to September 1864

ISBN/EAN: 9783744687508

Printed in Europe, USA, Canada, Australia, Japan

Cover: Foto ©ninafisch / pixelio.de

More available books at **www.hansebooks.com**

LETTERS FROM THE FRONT

FROM OCTOBER, 1861, TO SEPTEMBER, 1864,

BY

CYRUS MORTON CUTLER,

Of Lexington, Middlesex Co., Mass., while a member of Co. F 22nd
Massachusetts Volunteer Infantry Regiment and Battery C
1st New York (Light) Artillery Regiment.

"Haec juvabit olim meminisse."

THESE letters are arranged and published—Firstly, out of my love and respect for the memory of my dear brother, who followed the fortunes of the camps, campaigns and battles of the Army of the Potomac, during 1861-2-3-4, on whose record of service no higher enconium need be passed than that granted by all who served with him—"a good soldier and a faithful comrade" and to whose modesty and lack of self-interest alone, is due that absence of preferment and promotion, which though proffered, was never sought or accepted. Secondly, from a like love and respect for the memory of our father, whose national service during the War of 1812, and later, in the Volunteer Militia of his State, leads me to believe that the martial spirit—so rife in our grandfather, Thomas Cutler, of "Lexington Minute Men" and April 19, 1775 fame, as well as among our remote ancestors of Colonial days—slumbered during peace, only to arouse with renewed vigor, when arms were to be borne in the good cause; and, Finally, for my two sons, whom I trust, these "simple annals" of a "good soldier" will teach, how much is due to those who served and fought "that the Republic might live."

> "Their swords are rust—their bones are dust
> Their souls are with the saints, we trust."

A. D. CUTLER.

San Francisco, Cal., Oct., 1892.

The author of these letters, Cyrus Morton Cutler, was born January 18, 1841, on the homestead of his father and ancestors, who had occupied it since 1635, in Lexington, Massachusetts, being the eighth of eleven children (five sons and six daughters) of Leonard and Maria (Cutter) Cutler. He was a Massachusetts farmer's son, and as such, received the usual education and training, consistent with and common to his day and time. He enlisted in Co. F (Union Guard) 22nd Mass. Vol. Infantry, late in September, 1861, in company with three other of Lexington's sons, all of whom returned to their native town, at the expiration of their term of service, save one, who died of wounds received at Malvern Hill, Va.

He participated in all its experiences (save a short period in hospital during the Peninsula Campaign, 1862) until June, 1863, at which date he responded to a call for volunteers from the infantry to fill the depleted ranks of the light batteries of the Fifth Army Corps, being detailed to Battery C, First New York (Light) Artillery and serving with it as a private and non-commissioned officer until his muster out at expiration of the original 22nd's term of service in October, 1864. He was singularly fortunate in his exemption from disease and wounds, although constantly on duty, and is, recorded as being exceptionally reliable as to "good order and condition" and "present for duty."

Although not a frequent correspondent, his letters were graphic and full of descriptive strength, while his continued interest in family, friends and home matters were so prominent as to make him dearer than ever, and his safe return prayed for. Only those who lived during those stirring days can appreciate the hopes, fears and longings that followed our soldiers, and the joyous welcome accorded the briefest message from "the front;" and when the future historian shall write the true history of those days, he will gather no small measure of fact and inspiration from such letters from the "rank and file."

After his return to Massachusetts in 1864, his naturally adventurous spirit could not content itself with the peaceful home conditions, and led him to more stirring scenes. Firstly, to the newly discovered oil regions of Pennsylvania, and later to the broad plains of Kansas then being developed by the building of the overland railroads, with the construction of which and various cattle interests, he was connected until his death, probably about 1870, although the exact date is unknown in spite of many continued efforts to ascertain the facts.

Like many of his old comrades, he is debarred from the numerous happy affiliations of our late days, where the "Veterans of the Grand Army" are feted and honored, but our recollections of his youth are no less dear, or his record in his country's service no less bright, that he does not participate in those public recognitions of faithful service, that a grateful nation now happily bestows on his surviving comrades.

"The muffled drum's sad roll has beat the soldier's last tattoo;
"No more on life's parade shall meet the brave and fallen few.
"On fame's eternal camping ground their silent tents are spread,
"And Glory guards, with solemn round, the bivouac of the dead."

4

The 22nd Massachusetts Volunteer Infantry Regiment was organized under the patronage of its first colonel, Henry Wilson, then U. S. Senator, and later on, Vice-President of the United States, at Lynnfield, Massachusetts, and "mustered in" U. S. service "for three years or the war," October 8th, 1861, being ordered to Washington immediately thereafter and incorporated with the Army of the Potomac as part of the 1st Brigade, 1st Division, 5th Army Corps. It followed the fortunes of that Army for three and a half years, the original members being "mustered out" October 17th, 1864, and the remainder in July, 1865.

It participated in the following named general engagements as well as numerous others of less note:—Yorktown, Hanover Court House, Gaines' Mills, Malvern Hill, 2nd Bull Run (1st day), Antietam, Fredericksburg, Chancellorsville, Gettysburg, Mine Run, The Wilderness, Spottsylvania, North Anna, Bethesda Church, Cold Harbor, Assault on Petersburg (June 18, 1864), Siege of Petersburg, Hatchers' Run (2), Welden Road, Five Forks and the other final operations of the Army in March and April, 1865, preceding the surrender of the Confederate "Army of Northern Virginia." While it lost 279 men in killed and by deaths from wounds received in action, out of the total membership of 2078, it never relinquished its colors, save to the Governor of Massachusetts, on its return to the State, where they now hang in the Doric Hall of the State House, as a proud emblem and sacred memory of the past.

Company F was recruited largely in the neighboring town of Woburn, one of its members becoming a field officer of the Regiment, and its record was that of all the Companies of the 22nd and excelled by none. Its total membership was 139, and the losses—12 killed in action, 8 died from wounds and 9 from disease—29 in all.

The 1st N. Y. (Light) Artillery Regiment was organized in central New York in the Fall of 1861, and its Batteries (twelve) were scattered through the various Corps of the Armies of the Potomac, Ohio and Cumberland, mainly in the first named.

Battery C was organized at Elmira, N. Y., and "mustered in" Sept. 6th, 1861, and attached at various times to the Artillery Reserve, also to the 9th and 5th Corps, of the Army of the Potomac, and participated continuously, in all the campaigns until April, 1865, being "mustered out" June 17, 1865.

COL. A. D. CUTLER,

My Dear Colonel:—Your kind letter of the 30th of Sept. welcomed my arrival here lately on my return from my Summer and Fall roamings and enjoyments North and West.

I am glad to learn of your interest in the 22nd Regiment of Massachusetts Volunteers, and of your brother's connection with it. It was one of the many much loved and admired regiments of my old Division at Hall's Hill, Va., and of my old Fifth Army Corps of Peninsula, loved like all the others, for its unsurpassed good qualities, its excellent management, fine drill, discipline, unflinching devotion to duty under the most trying circumstances, and firmness in meeting its opponents, no matter how superior in numbers. At Hall's Hill, side by side with its sisters from Massachusetts, the 9th and 18th Regiments and 1st Mass. Battery, and others from Maine, Michigan, New York, Pennsylvania and Rhode Island, the Division received for its excellent parade and drill, the commendation of the Commanding General of the Army, as a model for the Army and a warning to the regulars lest they be excelled. That standing it maintained throughout the War and, though equalled by the high and noble qualities of other organizations, it was never surpassed in its good deeds and devotion and its sacrifices to the Union cause.

At the battle of Gaines' Mills in the firm and long struggle against the determined efforts of its near three times more numerous opponents, the 22nd Regiment lost its noble loved Commander Col. Gove, (as did the 9th Col. Cass) but though sad and great the loss, under the effect of his good teachings, it never flinched in the long years following in any of its trying struggles and duties and with its sister regiments and batteries of Massachusetts, the history and examples of its deeds and devotion to the Union's cause, will ever be a pride and example for other organizations of the State and the pride of the State itself.

Ever yours truly,

FITZ JOHN PORTER.

The Letters.

Dear Mother:

Thinking that you would be anxious to hear from me, I sit down in great confusion. We arrived here Friday about 11 A. M. pretty well used up, our journey being an uncommonly long and tiresome one. We left Boston about 4 o'clock, Tuesday P. M. and arrived in New York about 10 A. M. Wednesday. We received great cheers all along the road. We had refreshments passed through the cars at Springfield. Left New York 8 P. M. on a boat for Jersey City distant about 3 miles, then took the cars to the Delaware River across to Philadelphia. Here we were treated tip top by the Quakers, left here at 10 A. M. for Washington, arriving here Friday noon at 10 A. M. When within 10 miles of Washington, our engineer jumped off and refused to do duty any further, as the road had been taken by the Secesh. 3 days before. Upon this, Col. Wilson ordered us to equip ourselves immediately and be ready for fight as we supposed. We found two men in our Regiment who were capable of steaming us on to Washington, and on we went, expecting to see fun at any minute. In coming on we lost three men; two overboard and one on the cars. We are now quartered on Pennsylvania Ave., one of the principal streets of Washington, in sight of the Capitol and White House. I went over the Capitol yesterday; it is the finest building I ever witnessed. When looking at it, it seemed impossible that the hands of man could accomplish so fine an affair. It is now 2 o'clock P. M. and we have just received marching orders for Munsons' Hill about 15 miles distant. If this is the place, we shall be with the advance guard, as the Rebels have driven our force back to there within a few days. It is impossible for me to write any more, for the order has come to march.　　　　C. M. CUTLER.

P. S.—If you write, direct to Washington, D. C., 22nd Reg. Co. F. This was written among 200 men, all talking at once. We are off. Sling knapsack! A good fine Sunday!

———

HALL'S HILL, VA., Oct. 15, 1861.

Dear Brother:

We arrived in Washington, Friday about 10 A. M. and were quartered on one of the principal streets right in sight of the Capitol and White House. On Saturday, we marched through the principal streets and by the Capitol to give old Abe a chance to see us. He liked the looks of us so well that he gave us more credit than was due, and has thereby

sent us ahead of other regiments. The news came Sunday
that there was probably an engagement, as Gen. McClellan had
not returned to Washington on Saturday as usual. Capt.
Thompson came in about noon on Sunday and asked us boys,
"Are you ready for a fight?" and there was not one of us
that was not on his taps in less than a twinkle. He told us
to make ready to march at two o'clock, saying that we were
destined for Falls Church. We started and arrived here at
9 P. M. This place is ten miles from Washington south-west
of the Potomac. The ground that we occupy was in the
hands of the Rebs ten days ago. Their pickets now extend
to Falls Church which is five miles distant. They are retreating every day and will probably make a stand at
Manassas. It is almost impossible to tell when or where the
next battle will be fought as the Rebels keep retreating. We
could see signal lights thrown up all along their line last
night (Monday) in the direction of Falls Church. Five hundred men were detailed to chop the woods in this vicinity
yesterday. Everything was laid waste, corn-fields and houses. I helped to demolish a dwelling house this morning to
get boards to build a cook house of and to use in the tents
and I can now look at it from where I am writing. There
is not a door, window or board left in the place. Right op-
posite to our camp was a large chestnut wood, now there is
not a tree standing. On our right there is a regiment of
cavalry, on our left the 7th Maine boys are stationed. We
cannot look in any direction without seeing an encampment.
There are fifty regiments camped within three miles of us,
which makes things appear decidedly warlike. Do not know
whether we will stop here one day or two months. We are
liable to march at any hour. Do not go on guard without
being fully equipped to leave at any time. We all enjoy ourselves first rate, seventeen in a tent. Afternoon! Have been
doing fatigue duty and then left with a party of six. Visited
Col. Cass' regiment one half mile distant in sight of the
Rebels. They expect a brush at any minute. A battery
close by shelled a Rebel house, and it now lies in ashes.
Dress parade is coming off and I must leave. Direct to
Washington 22nd Mass. Vol.

    P. S. I write in great confusion. Give best respects to
all friends. On a cartridge box. C. M. CUTLER.

Dear Bell:

I will sit down to write for the third time and see if I
can get an answer from home. I wrote a fortnight ago to
James and have not received an answer yet. If you should
see the pile of letters our Orderly produces every night for
the boys of Co. F you would not wonder that I was anxious
for one.

How are you getting along at home? I have no doubt
you are desirous of hearing from me as often as possible,
as I am in the land of the Rebels. We are now in sight of
Falls Church which is about two miles distant. The Rebel
pickets came within six miles of this place, last Thursday.
We sent out 100 men; ten from each company. I did not
go myself, being on guard at home. They were gone forty-
eight hours, but did not bring in any prisoners. The 18th
Mass., stationed in our rear, took one Friday, that had been
taken before by the 2nd Maine. He will be taken care of
this time. We are in Porter's Division.

Monday, 28.

An officer of the regular Army; our Division was re-
viewed by McClellan and staff on Saturday. It consists of
3 brigades, 4 batteries, and 2 companies of cavalry; in all,
18,000. We had a sham fight as Mr. Hartwell calls it, but
probably on a larger scale then he ever dreamed of. You
can imagine us in a field of 25 acres, infantry in 3 columns,
each column stretching away for half a mile, the batteries on
our right, the cavalry on our left. All movements were made
on the double quick. We were led up to the engagement sometimes by Regiment, and sometimes by brigade, firing and
then retreating to load. I tell you, it was a smoky, stunning
old time. All the boys found fault with, it was not reality.
We gained the day at last with a loss of very few   We are
under very strict discipline and are on guard or drill most of
the time. We shall probably advance or go into some fort, as
it is very cold here nights. Last night, we had a very hard
frost. I hardly think it much colder where you are.

How does Fred get along being Boss? Tell him to
write and tell me how those hogs, and things in general are.
How I should like to step in and be with you all for a day !
I like soldiering very well, and should be well contented if
I thought the things were going all right at home. If you
or Mother want any money, you can get it of Russell on my
account, and I will make it all right with him. It is now
9 P. M., the boys are all stretched out and it is time for me
to do the same. We have a fire in the tent to-night, and it

11

is very comfortable. If I had a pie, I should go to bed all right. We have bread and coffee for a change twice a day, week in and week out. But if I have Thanksgiving in Charleston, S. C., I shall get something better. Don't view this with a critic's eye.

C. M. CUTLER.

P. S. Direct 22nd Regiment, M. V., Co. F care Capt. Thompson.

————

HALL'S HILL, VA., Nov. 2, 1861.

Dear Brother:

I received yours day before yesterday and was very glad to hear from you, it being the first one that I have received from home. I had just returned from being a picket, and nothing could be more welcome than news from home. We started early last Tuesday morning, 22 men from each company, 250 men in all from our Regiment. This number was detailed from five regiments each, so we numbered in all about 1100 men. We started with forty rounds of cartridges and two days' rations apiece. We went in the direction of Falls Church, five miles distant. About half of us were posted on and in the vicinity of the railroad leading to Leesburg and Manassas Junction. The rest went on to the head-quarters of the pickets, two miles off. This picket duty is very particular business, especially in the night. Each one is cautioned to keep his eyes peeled, and lay low as the enemy appear in different forms. One Williams, a Rebel who fights on his own hook, appears in the shape of a calf. He has been successful, and boasts how many men he has picked. He shot one of the Maine boys, three nights since, and wounded another in the hand. A bounty of $500 is offered for him by the government. Nothing of importance occured the first night. The next morning we were relieved by our reserve. We then acted as reserves and had salt horse and crackers given out. We did the best we could until night came on, when hens, geese and pigs in the vicinity had to suffer. In proof I send the enclosed. About nine in the evening we were ordered after the wagons which had been sent after hay and had not returned in due time. We went as far as Vienna, five miles beyond our pickets. We were fired into from the woods, the balls passing over our heads. We returned to quarters; started for home the next morning being out two and a half days, bringing in nothing except a few potatoes, chickens, etc. We are at the brigade drill every afternoon under Gen. Martindale. He is a very smart man and is bound to make us efficient in drill if possible. We

12

had something new yesterday which was, "Charge bayonets at double quick." This is done with a yell and is enough to scare the devil himself. It is raining very hard and has been all night. One half of our tents are nothing but mud. When it rains here it makes a business of it. I am sick of Hall's Hill and hope we shall make an advance. We were disappointed in not going on the naval expedition.

I am glad the hogs are doing well. When the steers get home, do as you think fit with them. Settle for them and the cow Esterbrook took. They went up the 25th of May. Tell Abbie those things in that bag are very useful. Tell Bell and Fred to write. Much love and respect to all. Fall in for dinner Co. F. Write soon.

C. M. CUTLER.

P. S. Send me a paper, if convenient.

HALL'S HILL, VA., Sunday, Dec. 22, 1861.
Dear Brother Fred:

I sit down to write you a few lines in answer to that letter which you wrote me. I hope that you will not feel slighted that I have not written before.

What are you doing with yourself, this winter? Going to school, I suppose. I often think of you getting up in the morning, going out to milk, and then coming in to a good hot breakfast. How you ought to value it. No one knows how to value a home until deprived of one, although I am satisfied to soldier as long as war continues. We rise in the morning at taps at 6:30 o'clock. All turn out for roll call. It would please you to see some of the boys hug their beds; but most of them manage to get out without hats or shoes which saves them from being checked. Then comes breakfast which consists of bread and coffee; then, we drill in the bayonet exercises for one hour; then we have a rest until 10 o'clock when company drill takes place till noon. In the afternoon from 2 to 5, we have battalion or brigade drill; then comes supper. Nothing is thought of after this time, except letters and papers from home. I do not think I received my complement of late. I wish you would write once a week how you prosper. How much milk are you making this winter, and how many cows are you keeping? What are you graining them on? Is George with you now? Since writing my last, I have been to Alexandria; it is quite a place. Went into the Marshall House and saw the place where Ellsworth was killed. The stairs on which he was shot

13

have been entirely cut away and carried off. I obtained a piece large enough to make a cane which I shall send home, if possible. Last Sunday I went over to Chain Bridge; it is quite a novelty. It is a quarter of a mile long, and is with a pile 60 feet above the water. The scenery at this place on the Potomac is very grand. Fort Ethan Allen defends the bridge on the Virginia side of the river. We have been very busy for three days back fixing our tents, palisading them; have a stove in ours which cost $7.00. The rest of the boys look upon us with envy, and even the officers come in to see us. Our division was reviewed yesterday by Gen. McClellan and staff. There is some talk of our going to South Carolina, but I hardly think so.

How does Wm. W. Hartwell survive the winter? Have you had much snow yet? We have not. Tell Mother the box of goodies has disappeared mysteriously. It sits close by, full of plates, canteens, dippers, a few blank cartridges, etc., etc. I found those letters enclosed; shall endeavor to answer them Tell all the folks to write.

From your brother,

C. M. C.

HALL'S HILL, Va., Jan. 1, 1862.

Brother Lewis:

I sit down to write you a few lines in answer to yours of Dec. 8th. First, I wish you and yours a Happy New Year, hoping that by the time another rolls round, it will find the country in different circumstances. Nothing of importance has happened of late. We went on picket last Saturday and returned on Monday. It was quite cold, but we managed to live through it. We took a darkey prisoner. Last night we heard heavy firing off towards McCall's Division, and have received news to be ready to move at a minute's notice; but I guess it will amount to nothing, as we very often receive like orders and have got used to them.

John Gleason has got an office which he has much sought after, which is to bring the grub from the Quartermaster's and deliver two candles to each tent. This relieves him from all guard duty. Oh! for an office! Corporal Lunt still sustains his position with credit to himself and town; he hails from A. Cotton still lives; he is the best shot in the company. We had a target shoot and he made the best shot; and if you believe me, I did the next at 150 yds. distant. We have the Enfield rifle; they kill at 1000 yds. We are to receive the U. S. Springfield rifle, considered the

14

best in the world, as those we have were made in too much of a hurry to be good.

I don't know how long we shall stay here; we have some chance of going South. There are all kinds of rumors round the camp and great betting about our destination. A week ago, we thought we should go to Fort Warren in Boston Harbor, but that is played out. Anything but Hall's Hill. I think there will be an advance on Richmond soon.

The other night, when on guard, the sentinel next beat to me, shot two of his fingers off. He was going double quick and fell down on his rifle, hand on the muzzle. It went off, taking the fingers close to the hand.

How is business with you? How does the Home Guard prosper? I am well, except a bad cold, which we are all troubled with. From your brother, C. M. C.

P. S.—Annie, I am much obliged for the goodies received from you. May God bless you. Brigade drill this afternoon.

———

HALL'S HILL, Va., Jan. 18, 1862.

Dear Bell:

I received yours and Fred's letter dated Jan 3d in due time. And as I suppose you will be looking for an answer, I will write, although I have nothing very interesting to communicate. We are still on Hall's Hill, up to our knees in mud and water. I was on guard night before last and on fatigue to-day, in the rain. This weather is giving us all colds. There are two out of our tent in the hospital; Watson of Woburn and Ed. Chandler, who is sick with fever. He has been quite sick; is better now. I shall see him to day; he will be out before long. I heard to-day that we shall not leave this place until we left for Mass. This is rather sickening for us who a week ago were expecting to go South any day; but it is all Col. Wilson's doings, who likes to have his pets where he can see them often, which he does, accompanied by his brother Reps. I will send you a picture of him. We are as comfortable as you could imagine in our rag houses. I invented a bunk and all the boys have followed suit. We are going on picket next Tuesday morning. You can think of me about that time looking out for Rebels. We shall be gone out two and a-half days; 500 out of the Reg. Last night after 10 P.M., there was a continual heavy firing off to the South of us, which was probably an attack on the rebel batteries on the lower Potomac. We expect to hear good news of Burnside's expedition. I should like to have gone with him.

Tell Fred, I left that dog-skin at the tannery on the

left, just before you get to the place called "The Foot of the Rocks;" small building in the rear. I should like to have you get it because I think it will make something quite nice.

Do you know that I am my own man this day? Twenty-one years old! Quite an old man; am I not, with my experience? I wonder what the next twenty-one years will bring me, if I live! Two years ago, I was in Ashby, Mass., working for Bradley; now, here I am in Va., working for Uncle Sam.

I received that Atlantic Monthly which I like very much. It helped to wear away many a lazy hour. Tell Mother to write me; I hardly hear a word from her. Ask her if she remembers the dinners she and I used to have last winter, about this time.

I will post you a Washington paper at the same time as this letter. Write and tell me if you have to pay postage on the letters you receive from me. When on guard, the sentry of the next beat to me shot two of his fingers off.

We shall be at home by next May.   From

C. M. C.

—————

CAMP WILSON, HALL'S HILL, Va., Jan. 30, 1862

Dear Bell:

I received your letter dated Jan. 19th about 9 A.M. Was out on picket at the time. We sent in two of the men after the letters, and with the rest, mine came which was quite unexpected as I had just sent one home which you have received before this time. You ask me in regard to my cold; I have got perfectly well of it. The weather out here is very bad of late. I have not seen the sun for three weeks; it is raining, hailing or snowing continually. The mud is very deep, from 6 to 12 inches, which makes it almost impossible to do much. The wagons are not allowed to go out without six horses each, the roads are so bad. Last week Friday, the orders came to march, pack up our extra baggage to send to Washington. We did so, but have not started yet and probably shall not until the 1st of Mar. We are not going on any naval expedition. When we move, we shall advance on towards Centreville and Manassas. Bull Run is twenty-five miles from this place. We have 250 pieces of cannon this side of the river which would be impossible to move at present. I have no doubt that the people at the North are impatient for a movement on the Potomac. I am myself; but if they were out here, they would be satisfied to the contrary. McClellan is waiting for settled weather, before he makes a movement. He would lose half of his men by sickness, if he broke camp now. One of the 2nd Maine who was on guard Tuesday night, died Wednesday with the cold he got.

In regard to clothing, I have a plenty. Fred said that Mother had a pair of mittens for me. I am just as much obliged as if I had none; but the Lieut.-Colonel was home at Boston and brought out mittens from the ladies for the whole of us. I want nothing so much as a pair of boots; but winter will soon be over with us.

Much love to all,
C. M. CUTLER.

P. S.—I saw Stevens, my old Woburn friend, when in N. Y. He treated me to pears to remind me of old times, a good dinner, filled my canteen, offered me money, etc. I forgot to tell you before, he asked for my sister and Miss Hartwell. He was in S. C. at the time of the Rebellion. Was offered a commission in the Rebel Army, but left for the North with his head.

CAMP WILSON, HALL'S HILL, Va., Feb. 7, 1862.
Dear Brother:

I received your letter Wednesday night and was very glad to hear from you. I have not got that letter you sent by Dr. Drew; probably he lost it and thought he would keep mum. We had a target practice this afternoon, six rounds apiece at 150 yds. I did not hit but once but it was as good as the average. The wind blowing very hard, you could not hold a gun steadily. Every fair day, our Brigade General puts us through to kill. Last Wednesday, our Brigade was on drill from 8 A.M. till 2 P.M. We had a sham fight; Follett's Battery and a Co. of Cavalry were present. Our Regiment was sent out as skirmishers. This is done to wake up the enemy and find their position. We deployed from the centre, the men being five paces apart; the Regiment reached a mile or more. After advancing about half a mile before we sighted the supposed enemy, we commenced firing. We retreated, then rallied on the reserve, then all fell back on the main body.

Sunday Eve., Feb. 9, '62. I left off writing to go on drill and have not had time since. Was on guard last night; got through with it first rate although rather cold. Have to go on once a week on account of half of our men reported unfit for duty. You speak of coming out here. I should like to have you tip top; but soldiering is not all fun. If you get out of biz., you had better take a trial of it. Variety

17

is the spice of life. The way things look now, I think the war will be settled soon; and if it is, I shall probably be out of it by the middle of summer.

I hope you do not think I am going to live in a rag house and lay on a rail for three years, not a bit of it. Uncle Sam can not stand it and will make mince meat of them before that time.

Russell has discharged me, and I am now my own man, or Uncle Sam's, I might say, if he wants me. Take a note from Mother for my share in the property. She might like to have me take it in wood which would release her from all interest and notes. You might take yours the same, if you choose; if not, I am satisfied to do otherwise. You speak of buying a milk route. I would if I were you; nothing like being boss of your own biz. I will help you what little I can when you are in want of the rocks. I should like to go in with you, if I were home.

Your truly,   C. M. CUTLER.

———

CAMP WILSON, HALL'S HILL, Va., Mar. 9, 1862.
My dear Bell:
It is Sunday afternoon after supper with us. It has been a very pleasant day, the most so, we have had since spring commenced. In the middle of the day, we can sit comfortably with both ends of the tent open. It is not so in Mass., as I hear by Messrs. Winn and Converse with whom I spoke yesterday. They are out here on a visit from Woburn. I heard directly from Abbie whom Mr. Converse saw a short time since. He speaks of the large quantity of snow you have. What a contrast! There is not a mite to be seen; the ground is thawed, the roads are getting settled fast, and the sacred soil of Virginia wears quite a different aspect from what it did a month since. I was on guard last night; the moon shone and it was warm as May.

Another man died to-day in the hospital belonging to our company. He has not been well since he has been here. We are going on picket tomorrow, which I hope will be the last before we leave Hall's Hill. You folks at home are probably tired of hearing of the forward movement of the Army of the Potomac. Not more so than the boys of the Bloody 22nd which name they have christened it, for fear they will never have a chance to win it. Gen. Banks has taken Leesburg which is fifteen miles distant from us.

Fifteen minutes later! I had to stop writing to receive two days' rations of coffee and sugar, which is six table-spoonfuls of each. Ask Mother if she don't think we are

18

bountifully supplied. Nothing of importance has transpired since I last wrote you. There were 1100 pairs of stockings sent to the Reg. from Mass. Each man had a pair.

Yours with much love, from your brother,

C. M. CUTLER.

P. S.—"Don't view this with a school-marm's eye, but pass the blots, etc., by." Hoping this will find you all in good health, as it leaves me. Tell Fred to write.

ALEXANDRIA, Virginia, Mar. 20, 1862.

Dear Bell:

I received yours and Fred's letters last Thursday night; they were very welcome, as I had not received one for some time. We were then at Fairfax Court House. Last Friday night, our Brigade received marching orders for this place which is 18 miles distant. We started early Saturday morning in the rain (as it usually does) and arrived at Camp California, wet to the skin. This place is two miles out of the city. Yesterday we were selected as the Regiment to do provost guard for the city. It is quite an honorable position and all the better for us, as we have good quarters in the basement of a church. There are two companies in the body of the church and the same in the gallery. We shall probably stop here until the expedition which is now fitting up, gets off. There is some talk of our going to Washington on the same duty, after that; but hope not, as I should rather go South with our Division, which is in Heintzleman's Corps. The river is full of steamers and transports loading with coal and provisions with all dispatch.

You ask me how spring opens here. It is getting to be quite warm. I should judge that it was six weeks earlier than Mass. The buds on the trees are swelling and the leaves will shortly be out. We have not had our tents since we left Hall's Hill, Mar. 10. Since that time each man has had to cook his own grub, which has been quite a task for us as dishes are very scarce. Every place we go we are minus something. ' I have nothing but a quart dipper, for which I am very thankful, for quite a number of the boys have lost their knapsacks. One fellow from Reading has lost everything, gun and all. Ed. Chandler is getting to be dissipated in eating; does nothing but fry pork and hard bread until it has settled in his legs and he has to wear a shoe on one foot and boot on the other.

Via! I received that box containing the nice pair of

boots and a good pair of stockings, night before last. They were very acceptable indeed. Lieut. Crane carried the box round some time trying to find me, and he has been worried about it as it was particularly in his charge.

Yours truly, with much love to all,

C. M. CUTLER.

BIG BETHEL, Va., Mar. 26, 1862.

Dear Mother:

As I have some spare time, I think I will pencil you a few lines to let you know where we are. Since I last wrote, we have made quite a move. We were then at Alexandria. Our Division embarked last Friday afternoon and started down the river next morning, arriving at Fortress Monroe late Sunday night. We had a first rate trip having good weather all the way down. Our Regiment had the " Daniel Webster," a large ocean steamship of 1300 tons. Among the others were the " Milley Baker " and " Nantasket " from Boston, which reminded me of old times. Fortress Monroe is the finest piece of work of the kind I ever saw. There are seventy-five acres enclosed within the walls, laid out with walks, shade and fruit trees all over it. The walls are built for two tiers of guns. There is a ditch of about 25 feet entirely round it whose bank is nicely grassed over. I saw the big Union gun which weighs 40,099 lbs. and carries a solid shot of 600 lbs. They are just mounting her so as to command the entrance of James River. By the way, I suppose you have heard of the engagement between the Merrimac and Monitor. That little craft, if so I may call her, is a big thing on a small scale. She is built so as to be very little exposed, is but between two and three feet above water, except her wheel-house and cheese box, all of which are built of plate iron. She draws eleven and a half feet of water, is perfectly tight on deck, and therefore, can never sink. I saw the shot they use aboard of her. They are wrought iron between 200 and 300 lbs. weight. The Government have two more, building, like her which will be accomplished shortly. If the Merrimac comes down the river, she will probably meet with a warm reception. I hope you will not get tired reading this.

We left Fort Monroe Monday noon and marched to Hampton, five miles distant. This place was burned by the Rebels last Aug., when they left it. The 16th Mass. is encamped here, the one that Charley Cutler is in. I did not have time to see him, but heard from him by way of one of his company. We left there yesterday morning and

20

arrived here in the afternoon. We are probably on our road
to Richmond. Capt. Sampson's Company was fired into
this morning on picket, about 40 rods from camp. Our
sharpshooters are out looking after Rebels. I write this
lying between two sacks of wheat which I am guarding. We
came past a peach orchard yesterday, which was just bloom-
ing out.   From your son,

                                C. M. CUTLER.

NEAR YORKTOWN, Va., Apr. 21, 1862

Dear Brother:

As I have not heard a word from you for over two
months, you will not wonder at my writing again. I have
written to you twice and have not had an answer to either.
You have doubtless heard of our departure from Hall's Hill
through the columns of the Woburn Budget. We have
been at this place a fortnight last Saturday. For the last
ten days, I have been on fatigue duty, building bridges and
fortifications. Our Division have built six bridges across a
stream running into the York River regiments relieving
each other both day and night. Yesterday, Sunday, we
turned out at 4 o'clock in the morning, and were detailed to
work on a breastwork which will mount twelve heavy guns
directly in sight of the Rebels, but screened from them by a
lot of brush thrown up for the purpose. While we were
digging, one of the boys found a 10 lb. shot which was fired
in an engagement between the English and Americans
eighty-one years ago. Day before yesterday, I went over to
the 2d N. H., Hooker's Division, about half a mile distant.
Saw Fred Cutler; he did not know me, but I knew him the
minute I got my eyes on him, He has not changed a mite;
is the same old sixpence. He had a great many questions
to ask in regard to the girls of the Cutler family; who was
married and who wasn't, etc., etc., edifying me an hour or
so with his usual amount of fox stories.

Tell Abbie those stockings that accompanied the box
were just what I wanted and came in the right time.

What are you doing at home? I expect to hear something of you soon; gone to the war, bought a milk route or
got married. The ball will open here in five or six days.
I have not time to write more. The fruit trees are all in the
height of bloom.   From your brother,

                                C. M. CUTLER.

21

Mrs. Cutler:

Yours of the 20th reached me day before yesterday at our camp near Barker's Mill. The letter you sent to Morton is also in my charge. I shall keep it until I find out where he is now. I have made several efforts to find out whether he is still at West Point, Va., or has been sent to some northern hospital on board of a U. S. Transport, but as yet have been unable to learn anything definite or satisfactory. Our Asst. Surgeon, Dr. Prince, the ablest man in our medical department, was left in charge of our sick boys at West Point, where we left Morton; and if he be still there, he has good care taken of him. Our surgeon has left us on account of sickness, so that it is difficult now to ascertain anything about matters in his department. On our regimental books, our sick, left behind, are reported from day to day: "Absent, sick." That gives me no information, so I have just written a letter to the commander of the Post at West Point to ascertain, if possible, his whereabouts and situation. Perhaps he may have reached home by this time (I hope he has); but I shall not abate my efforts until I learn how and where he is. Our many and rapid marches since we separated, have made it impossible to keep up communication. It is more difficult to hear from West Point, although only 35 miles distant, than it is from Massachusetts, as there are no mail accommodations between here and the former place. I shall send by private conveyance and all that can be done for his comfort by me shall be cheerfully done for the love I bear him. He was in good spirits when I saw him, and expressed the hope of joining us soon, as he then felt that he should be nicely in a few days. He promised me that he would write you soon and often. I presume he has. We all felt bad about his being obliged to remain behind, and hope to see him in our ranks again as cheerful and lively as ever. If you think of anything that I can do, please command me, for I am at your service.

. The Rebels are drawn up in line of battle within sight of our camp. We are now nine miles from Richmond, by the road, and hope to be in the Rebel capital soon. Hoping that a speedy victory and an honorable peace will soon enable us all to return to our friends, I remain, respectfully yours, etc.,

J. FRANK GLEASON,

Co. F 22d Mass. Regt. Vol.

Fairfax St. Hospital, Alexandria, Va., 5-29-1862.
Dear Isabella:

Thinking that you would be somewhat anxious to know where I am and my situation at present, I thought it best to inform you. I was brought to the hospital at this place on the 14th, sick with fever. I came by boat from West Point. I was in the hospital there or in that vicinity at that time and was too sick to be a participant. I was four days in coming here, and during that time received no attention scarcely; but I found quite a comfortable place here, a good physician, kind female nurse, and male attendants equally good and kind, and through their attendance and treatment medically, I received, I find myself now recovering, and hope ere long to be fit again for the duties of the field. I have strength sufficient to walk across the room, but am in bed yet a good part of the time. Time drags away slowly here, but I am glad I am so comfortably situated. Tell Mother she need not be worried about my sickness, as I am not dangerous and am well taken care of, and will soon be well. I wish James would write to me. I have not received a letter from him for two months, and now when I am sick, I think he should write. I have money enough to procure me any little necessaries that I need. I hope that this will find you all in good health and giving yourself no uneasiness in regard to me. All I ask of you is to write as soon as possible. My love to all.

Direct to your loving brother,

C. M. CUTLER.

———

Alexandria, Va., June 19, 1862.
Dear Brother James:

I received your letter dated the 16th yesterday, and one from Bell by the same mail besides a word from S. A. Gardner. The boys envied me as I was the only one that received any in our ward, as letters are a great rarity out here these long days. There are 130 patients in the hospital. The Mansion House has 1410 in it. Some Secesh put a barrel of powder under this building and would probably have blown it up had not the patrol discovered it. They are getting very bold of late, having shot two Union soldiers yesterday. They were taken up and put in the slave pen, where they will probably have time to meditate. You speak of my coming home. It is impossible to get a furlough. I see it tried every day. And more so in this Hospital than in some others, unless you have some disease and are disabled, there is no getting home. I wish I was able to go to my Regiment, as it is like being in prison here. We can not get out without a pass from the Dr. He would not give me one, but I made out to get out yesterday. I am getting better every day, and hope to be with the boys within another month. Give my love to Joseph and Abbie and the children. From your ever loving brother,

C. M. C.

P. S.—I see you have not changed your business yet. Very well! A rolling stone gathers no moss; a sitting hen lays no eggs. Wait until this miserable war is over.

ALEXANDRIA, Va., June 20, 1862.

My dear Mother:

I received Bell's kind letter dated the 15th inst. I was very glad to get it as it brought such good news and remembrances of home. How I should like to be there again! But it is useless in trying to get a furlough. One of the boys that came here the same time I did and has had a fever, asked the Doctor yesterday for one. He said there was no such thing in the book. In fact, it is no use asking for one, as we always get the same answer. Tell Bell she ought not to speak of beefsteak, pies, etc., to a soldier, as those are things we know nothing of. I showed the letter to some of the boys; they advised me to show it to the Dr. To tell the truth, Bell can't be beaten in writing letters. I am getting along as fast as could be expected; am very hearty, eating my rations, with a pint of milk and crackers, or something of the kind, at the table of a nice old lady, the other side of the street at my own expense. You see I am bound to live, if I am among the Secesh. We are not allowed to go out without a pass from the Dr., only across the street after milk. This makes it bad for us, but we manage to get what we want by dropping a little fellow (a Captain's servant) out of a back window some six feet to the ground, for which consideration he gets numerous cakes. I have been here now over a month, and am tired and sick of the place. I hope by another I will be all right; but have got to eat some in the time to do it. I should like to come home very much, as I find the longer I live and the more I see, there is no such place elsewhere; and if we ever get through this miserable Rebellion, I intend to have one. But I never want to leave where I am until it is over, if I can have my health; not because I like it, but because I think it the duty of every one now engaged to take hold and end it as quickly as poss-

24

ible. I think by cold weather things will be straightened, so some of the regiments will be discharged.

I think by what Fred wrote me of his farming, that he is doing first rate; better than could be expected of him; but then, the Cutler boys can do anything they take hold of.

How does Mr. Hartwell bear the cares of life? I hear very little from him. I suppose he is hoeing his corn and potatoes as usual. I wish I was doing the same thing. The season down here is very backward, although the market is well supplied with strawberries, cherries, tomatoes, etc. The peaches are as large as pullets' eggs.

The Hospital is close by the Potomac. We can look over into Maryland and see the green wheat fields, which make one think of something besides war. Take good care of yourself, and do not use your lame arm, and do not worry yourself about things. I shall except a word from you soon. I have been all day writing this, as I had to give up the pen.

By the way, my knapsack turned up to-day. One of the boys found it. It looked like an old friend.

From your son,

C. M. CUTLER.

HARRISON'S LANDING, Va., Aug. 14, 1862.

Dear Mother:

I hope you will forgive me for not writing before, but it is so warm that one has enough to do to keep cool without speaking of anything else. I returned from the Hospital a fortnight ago and am now in good health, feeling first rate and hope this will find you the same. We are encamped close to the river, where we can enjoy a good wash with pleasure. And men are pretty well played out with the heat and fatigue they have been through. The Regiment now numbers 218 men, instead of 1250 which came out. Lieut. Crane and five men that were taken prisoners to Richmond, returned this week. They looked hard, having suffered everything but death, the Rebs. having starved them. There is a great secret movement at hand of which nobody, except the head officers, have any idea and when. Knapsacks were sent down river three days ago. We are now in light marching order, expecting to move any time the opportunity comes. The Rebs. are too strong for us at this position, and "Mack" is withdrawing his forces as best he can, keeping up appearances at the same time. How does J. Gleason carry sail? The men of the Co. are all down on him, because of the way he got home. It takes a sharp man to get out of a scrape; one that has been to college.

How does Fred get along with the haying? I suppose he is nearly done by this time. I often think of him sweating away in the meadows. How does neighbor Hartwell prosper? Does he get any of his hay wet? Give my best respects to him. I hope you do not lose any sleep on my account. I did, my bed having broken down three times last night. How does your arm get along? Be careful and take care of yourself. From your ever loving son,

C. M. CUTLER.

Bad news. Chandler ate his last box of sardines yesterday, having had his pocket picked of all he had, $18.50.

SHARPSBURG, Md., Sept. 29, 1862.

My dear Bell:

I received your letter of the 11th inst. last night, and as you find paper, I can not do less than to answer it. The last time I wrote home, we were at Hall's Hill expecting to stay there in defense of Washington. But there is no rest for us. We marched some 125 miles since then. Our Brigade arrived here on Tuesday, the day before the Wednesday fight (Antietam). I fell out on account of sore feet the day before, but fell in with the 5th Maine Regiment, Franklin's Corps, as I could not find any of Porter's, and was with them all day. The fighting was tremendous from sunrise to sunset. During the afternoon, we drove them about a mile which gave us a good chance to see what our batteries had done for them. The ground was completely covered with their dead and wounded. It was an awful sight, but such is war. The battle-ground was north-west of the Cumberland Mts., as handsome a country as ever you saw, as is all Maryland we have passed through, entirely different, as the Va. people and everything else. I joined my Regiment the next day, finding they had not been in the fight, they acting as a reserve. The Saturday following, our Brigade forded the river near Shepardstown. We had barely got across and thrown out the 118th Pa. Regiment as skirmishers, when the Rebs. came down on us in force. We came back in a hurry, each one looking out for himself. We got across losing but two men. The other Regiment and the Brigade suffered a great deal more. The 118th Pa. lost 150 men, as they were the last to cross. Since then, we have been doing picket duty on the Maryland side of the river near Shepardstown and can see the Rebel flag flying there. Ed. Chandler went over to see his big brother Sam who brought me word from you.

Via! John and Adam Peters were both wounded in the late battle. E. Fisk's brother was killed. Cousin Fred Cutler was wounded in the head and foot at the battle of Bull Run (second) bringing off a prisoner when he came off the field. Chandler wishes me to say that he is all right, ready to make another raid into Virginia, as is your humble servant and affectionate brother,

C. M. CUTLER.

P. S.—In regard to the box, do not send till we go into winter quarters, as we lose everything on our marches.

FALMOUTH, Nov. 25, 1862.

Dear Brother:

I received yours yesterday, Sunday, and was very glad to hear from you. I suppose the folks at home, especially Abbie and Nell, think I have forgotten them because I do not write. We have been continually on the move since leaving Maryland. We are now under General Joe Hooker, the old fighting cock, and expect to see some fun before long. The Rebs. occupy Fredericksburg about one and one half miles from here, and as soon as the bridges running to Acquia Creek are reported open, we shall move in that direction. It is getting to be very cold down here, I wish you would send me a pair of woollen gloves by mail. We had a snow storm on the 7th of the month, water freezing in our canteens every night. Pretty cold weather for the new recruits, $150 men, $50 men, $25 men. I congratulate you and all the rest of the folks on a good turkey dinner. I will be with you in thought, if not in person. How is mother, at home? Write and tell me all the news, your future prospects, etc., etc. I am in good health and hope this will find you the same. Give my love to Abbie and Joseph. From your ever loving brother,

C. M. CUTLER.

NOTE —A very interesting letter, descriptive of the Battle of Fredericksburg, Va., Dec. 13, 14 and 15, 1862, cannot be found. A. D. C.

NEAR FREDERICKSBURG, Va., Jan. 27, 1863.

Dear Brother:

I received your letter to-night, and as I am not much inclined to sleep, I will favor you with a few lines. A week

27

ago to-day, Tuesday, we started to cross the river, but got stuck in the mud. Gen. Siegel was to take the advance, but, as the rainy weather commenced, it proved a failure; nothing of importance helped. We were out four days getting wet to the skin. The first night did not sleep a wink, often getting back the artillery and baggage wagons by corduroying the roads. We returned to camp where I hope they will be willing to let us rest.

Jan. 31, 1863. Since commencing this, our Brigade has been on picket; was out four days, seven miles towards Warrenton. It rained when we started out which turned into snow, which fell for about a foot, the most I have seen in Virginia. It was beautiful coming in, the mud, water and snow up to our knees. A great many of the men are sick. The recruits are getting their discharges very fast. One Hamilton of our Company, who says he is acquainted with you and has taken milk of you in Charlestown, is very low and will probably get his discharge. Cy. Converse of Woburn got his to day. The 22d number 204 guns. The Army generally is discouraged and demoralized, having not received any pay for the last six months. But we shall soon get some, as Maj. Holmes has arrived and with him, no doubt, a plentiful supply of greenbacks. Mr. Hackett came to light three days ago, bringing my package in good order. Tell Mother the stockings remind me of home, and I am very much obliged for them. We are very well supplied with stockings, as the Company received a hundred pairs from the ladies of Woburn, which gave each man three pairs. I am not in need of anything. I wish you would send me Boston papers, as reading matter is very scarce out here. G. Harrington is driving an ambulance. Ed. Chandler is regaling himself at the convalescent camp, Alexandria.

NEAR FREDERICKSBURG, Va., Feb. 7, 1863.

Dear Brother:

We were paid a few days ago. I send you by express $60.00 with which you do as you think proper. I am in good health, with the exception of a cold; but am heartily sick of the war, as are all the boys, and shall get out of the service at the first opportunity. Everything seems to go against us of late. Joe Hooker has command of the Army now, and the next movement, you may expect to hear of a failure, as none of us have any confidence in his generalship.

How are Nell and Frankie? I should write, but am

28

such a poor hand at it, and do not feel in the mood
very often.

I lost all papers and accounts you sent me. They were
taken out of my knapsack. From your brother,

C. M. CUTLER.

———

POTOMAC CREEK, Va., Feb. 20, '63.
Dear Bell:

I received a letter from you last night which I was very
glad to get, as the times are very dull out here and
anything from home is welcome. You speak of the want of
something more interesting to write. Do not let that trouble
you, for it does not me in the least. I was greatly surprised
the other day by Mr. Twombley and his father-in-law making their appearance. They came quite a distance to see me,
and were much fatigued, having had a good introduction to
Virginia mud. Mr. T. was very anxious to see Fredericksburg, the battle field, etc., etc. Though raining hard, we
started on a reconnoissance for the above-named places, of
which we soon came in sight, with a few butter-nuts mixed
in, of which he was quite shy. He was much pleased with
what he had seen, and said that it paid him for his journey
from Massachusetts. We got back at 9 P.M. They stopped
over night in as good a bunk as the Army of the Potomac
can boast of and left in the morning for Fort Monroe. I
should have thought that Joseph or James would have come
with them. Tell them it is not too late.

Part of the Army has left here for further south; probably Newbern. Our destination is here until after the
contemplated fall of Vicksburg and Charleston. I think
(this is my own proposition) Richmond is to be left until the
last, when its fall will be terrible before the efficient Army
of the Potomac. Mr. Hackett arrived about a fortnight ago
bringing me the bundle which you sent. The shirts, hand-
kerchiefs and stockings were just what I needed, and for
each I am very much obliged. The stockings reminded me
of those worn in former days. We lately received three pair
per man from the ladies of Woburn. Long may they live!

Via! I hear Elise is married. Long may she live! We
are getting soft bread four times a week per order Gen. Joe
Hooker. Ed. Chandler is still in the hospital at Alexandria.
J. F. Gleason is at work at the Quartermaster's. Since the
battle of F., he has been reduced to $13.00 and one month's
pay stopped; but he is a good fellow.

Tear this up. I am in good health. Give my love to
Mother.

29

Dear Abbie:

You must excuse me for not writing before. We have been continually on the move since Joseph left me. The Rebs. have been on hand driving our outer pickets in every night or two, which, with a review by Gen. Hooker, has taken up most of the time. I was very sorry you did not make your appearance the next Sunday. I was looking for you all day, and did not give you up until Monday night, at which time I suppose you were on the way to Ft. Monroe. I was disappointed as well as the rest of the boys; for the pleasant countenance of a woman in camp would have been hailed with great pleasure. I had chartered a wall tent for your reception, which I am sorry you were not present to occupy.

Via! How did you like the looks of what you saw of old Virginia? Not very well, I guess. If you had seen as much of it as I have, you would not think it worth while to describe. I received the letters you wrote me in Washington and went over to Hooker's headquarters where I obtained the box without any trouble, and am much obliged to you and Joseph for the contents which were tried by all my tent's crew with Day and Sergeant Meriam who rung in. John Gleason said if I did not give him some of that butter he'd tell Abbie: but I didn't see the point.

Everything remains the same as it has for a long time. We received new dress coats in which the Regiment made quite an appearance at the late review, and are to get knapsacks soon. Furloughs are stopped. The women are all ordered from the Army by the first of April which looks like stirring times ahead. Let it come! The men are in good spirits. Joe Hooker has fed us well and gained the good will of all. I still remain in a house with sheeting for a roof and the ground for a floor.

I remain, your loving brother,

C. M. CUTLER.

Sunday afternoon. Col. Tilton, 22d Mass. Regiment; Gen. Barnes, 1st Brigade; Gen. Griffin, 1st Division; Gen. Meade, 5th Army Corps.

———

NEAR FREDERICKSBURG, Va., May 10, 1863.

Dear Bell:

As I know you will be anxious to hear from me at the present time, I will write a few lines. The Army fell back across the Rappahannock on the night of the 8th inst.

in a drizzling rain with mud about six inches deep; for what reason remains to be found out. It is said that the cause of the failure is laid to the 11th Army Corps, composed entirely of Germans, who broke and confused the whole thing. Never was there an army started in better spirits than ours did the 29th of April. Underwent every fatigue without a murmur, confident of success. The first day we marched some twenty-seven miles to Kelly's Ford, where we stopped for the night; crossed on pontoons the next morning. About night, we forded the Rapidan, which was nearly up to our armpits. It was a laughable sight to see us crossing divested of all our clothes except our shirts. Slung about our necks, were eight days' rations; but it was more prose than poetry, I assure you, as the current was very swift. The 5th Corps arrived there just in time to avoid a battle, as the Johnnies were making for it on the other side. We lay down much elated at our success that night. We came up with them the next morning and drove them from their rifle pits which they were building all night. That day was spent in reconnoitering and forming lines of battle. The next day the 11th Corps broke when the Rebs. charged, which brought the 5th to the front, which we held for five successive days and nights. The Rebs. charged on us repeatedly day and night, but our grape and canister were too hot for them. Never were there men acted more recklessly than they, marching out in solid columns over and over again when we mowed them down like grass. On Sunday, after coming out several times, they set the woods on fire, the wind being the right way to drive the smoke in our faces, and advanced under cover of that, but were repulsed with great loss. Just at this time, Gen. Hooker was unhorsed by a piece of spent shell; Gens. Berry and Whipple were also killed. Our loss is small, on account of being behind the breastworks. I will send you a piece of conical shell from the Rebs. which came within close proximity of your humble servant. With love,

C. M. CUTLER.

Give my love to Mother. Tear this up; for I shall not write, if my letters are heralded all over the State.

BEVERLY FORD, Va., Aug. 10, 1863.

My dear Mother:

I have not heard from home for some time, although I have written several letters. I shall soon begin to talk the way Bell talks to me. It's a poor rule that will not work both ways. We are now taking a little rest, if there is such a thing as rest. This warm weather it is almost impossible to stop out in the sun. Quite a number of men have been sunstruck walking their beat. This place is about 15 miles south of Warrentown. We are close by the river where the pontoons are laid. I do not know whether it is the intention to move us across or not, but do not think it likely, as report says that Lee intends to make another raid on Washington. I hope this is so; if he does, it will be the last of his Army. His combined forces will be too much for us; but as he can not enter the place without losing half his strength, and can not stay there if he takes it, it will be like going to Pa. Everything looks favorable to us down here, and if we can only take Charleston, it will be the biggest thing yet. Richmond, we are leaving for the last, when all the boys are going to take a hand, the conscripts included, and make short work of it.

Where is James? I have not heard a word from him for the last three months. I received a letter from Russell with news altogether better than I expected concerning my pecuniary affairs, etc.

How does the haying prosper? How I should like to take a week or so in the hay-field! But I think Fred would be more than a match for me, as I am such a veteran I have forgotten everything about farming I ever knew; and "action to front, limber to rear," has become second nature to me. I like the Artillery much better than the Infantry. There are but twenty-five of the original men in this Battery; the rest are made up from the Infantry. There are four of the 22d here, and some from the 12th and 13th Mass.; Maine, N. H., Vt. and Pa. regiments are represented here, also. The captain was a minister, but has descended a grade or two like all army officers. I am pretty well, but feel a little touch of the fever I had last summer.

I want you to have your picture taken for me. Tell James to write. From your son,

C. M. CUTLER.

BEVERLY FORD, Va., Aug. 22, 1863.

Dear Brother:

I send you by express to-day $40.00. I received your letter in due time. The statement was altogether better than I expected. We are lying close by the river in the face of the Rebs. We expect them to open on us at any moment, but we are well prepared. I like the artillery much better than the infantry. I am well. Give my love to Nell.

Your obedient servant,

C. M. CUTLER.

BEVERLY FORD, Va., Sept. 13, 1863.

Dear Brother:

I received Bell's letter yesterday. I have not had one before for nearly a month. The one with the stamps, I did not get. We received marching orders this morning, but Corps has already crossed the river, and by the sound of the artillery, have come upon the Rebs in the direction of Culpepper. This may not be more than a reconnoissance to find out where they are, as everything has been very quiet of late on both sides; but I think it is preparatory to a general move. We received news last night that Charleston, S. C., was taken. I hope so, but hardly think it possible so soon. We lie in the same position we have for a month back, watching the Reb's signal fires every night. It rained yesterday for the first time for a month. I was over to see the 22d which lie up the river two miles. Geo. Harrington is back having gone to the hospital before the battle in Pa. He had the misfortune to have a wagon run over his foot in Maryland. My old tent mate, Ed. Chandler, is in the Invalid Corps at Washington. He sends me a paper every now and then. He has not been with us since last fall at Sharpsburg. You will soon hear from J. Gleason.

The 29th of Aug., I was present at the execution of five privates of the 118th Pa. Vol. It was a very solemn affair; the whole Corps were present to witness it. They were marched from the guard house each man behind his own coffin, the whole length of the Corps, the band playing a funeral note, and then to their graves which already were dug. They all fell dead at the word fire and were soon under the sod, a warning to all deserters.

My Regiment's time is up the 1st of Oct., 1864. The Battery's time is up the middle of Sept., 1864. We are attached to the Pa. Reserves, better known as the Bucktail Rifles 3rd Division 5 A. C.

Address hereafter Battery C 1st N. Y., Artillery Brigade 5 A. C., Washington, D. C., and I shall get all.

From your brother,

C. M. CUTLER.

Dear Brother:

I received Bell's letter last night, the first one for some time; also, one from Russell. James seems to have so much to attend to that he can not do much else. We are making ourselves quite comfortable in our winter quarters, with plenty to eat and just enough to do to make us feel well, each man having two horses to water, feed and exercise. Enlisting over again is all the go here. Over thirty of the men belonging to the Battery have signed their names in hopes of the furlough, the big bounty, etc.; but the afterclap sticks in my crop (3 years more) and as yet, I am on the fence preferring to serve out this term before getting in any deeper; but may change my mind; as I think this war will be closed by next fall. .

It has been very cold for the last few days, which kept us pretty well engaged in keeping the fires good. There are three of us tent together; Bronson Felt, Joseph Grey and your humble servant. The last named and myself indulge in six blankets, two overcoats for a bed. Do you not envy us? Yesterday, there was a deserter shot belonging to the 7th Regular Infantry. It was in sight of camp, but I did not go to see it, as it has got to be an old story.

Bell tells me you are donning my coat, etc. I can hardly believe that you can have grown so. I am about the same as I was when I left home, and shall hardly dare to make my appearance next fall if you continue so. Give my love to Mother, and tell her I am glad she sold that wood. Tell her to use the money freely to make herself comfortable. The ration of candle is about gone; Brons has gone to bed; Joe is on guard, and I have the bed to make, so goodby for this time. Send me a Boston Herald, once in a while.   C. M. CUTLER.

Address 5th Army Corps, when you write, as this Regiment of Batteries has companies in every corps.

———

NEAR RAPPAHANNOCK STATION,

Battery C., 1st N. Y. Art'y. Sunday, Dec. 13. 1863.

Dear Sister Bell:

I received yours and Fred's letters, also Fred's letter containing the auction bill; but you must excuse me for not writing before, as we have been very busy of late building winter quarters. We have not got them half done yet, as we have to wait for each other, as the tools are very scarce. We have got the logs up and also the chimney, which has been a week's work, but begins to look as comfortable as you can imagine to us who have not had a bed twice in a place since last April. But Uncle Sam is going to give us a rest by present appearances, until he has use for us next spring.

Since I last wrote, our Battery has been in two little brushes with the Rebs.; one on the north bank of the Rapidan, and the other at Mine Run. We sustained no loss, except a wheel from one of the pieces, which was taken off by a shell at the last named place. We expected a big engagment at this place; but as the Rebs did not want to fight on fair terms, Meade declined fighting them at all. On Monday, the 30th of November, the Artillery which was in position for about three miles in front of the Rebs' entrenched works, was ordered to open on them at 8 A.M. This was done along the whole line, every one expecting them to reply in good earnest, but were somewhat surprised when we did not get but now and then a shot from their works, which were of great strength and fairly shone with cannon. This was kept up for about an hour and a half, when orders came to cease firing. They were waiting for some of our Infantry to come out so they could get up a second Fredericksburg affair; but on account of the cold and short rations, Meade slipped out that night. Our horses were without feed three days. Quite a number of them died of starvation. We had but four hardtack a day. The Infantry men were round trying to buy it, offering $5 a dozen; but there was none to be had. But everything is forgotten now; we are getting our soft tack and fresh beef in plenty, and everyone is getting fat.

Fred says in his last, I have not got enough of soldiering, that I am going to stop in the Army until the war is over. He draws a wrong conclusion from my statement. As soon as nine months more roll round, if I am all right, I shall return home. If I come in the Army again, it will be in another capacity than a soldier.

I am glad Mother concluded to sell off some wood, and hope she will appropriate some of the proceeds to her own use. I should judge by the figures that it sold very high.

Do not let this letter go out of the house; remember.

C   M.   CUTLER.

———

Sister Bell:

I received your letter three days ago, and will answer it now as I have an opportunity. An order came this morning that we could not send any mail for twenty days after today; and as I believe I am behind on correspondence with you, I will just let you know that I am well, etc. There is very little to write about.

We broke camp yesterday morning and crossed the Rappahannock. All the army seem to be getting ready for a move. We were relieved at Bealeton by a Mass. Battery, who expect to stop there this summer to guard the railroad. It was not our luck to get this chance; but for my part I'd rather be in the front than anywhere else, as the excitement and moving help to pass away time. I am never easy unless I am where the noise is going on. We are now stopping with the Reserve Artillery, and are not assigned to any Corps. There are some twenty-five batteries in this corps subject to be used where they are needed. The cars are coming in here every hour loaded with cattle, hardtack and pork, which is a petty sure sign of moving.

You must excuse me for closing so, but it sprinkles and I must fix the tent or lie in the water to-night. Give my love to Mother and Fred and all the rest. I forgot to tell you that the sutler got burned out the night before we left. His loss was some $9000 in goods and $4000 in greenbacks. No insurance! He barely escaped with his life which was not of much account. Supposed to be the work of an incendiary.

I received a letter from S. Gardner. He is in the 124th Ill. Regiment, Vicksburg.

Glory hallelujah!

From your affectionate brother,

C. M. CUTLER.
Address Battery C 1st N. Y., Artillery Reserve.

———

Near Petersburg, Va., June 21, 1864.
Dear Mother:

I think I will write you a few lines to let you know that Battery C is all right and that your humble servant is the same. We are in the fourth line of entrenchments that we have taken from the Rebels, and can see the steeples of Petersburg, but the Lord knows when we shall get there. Our Infantry is some two hundred yards in advance of us behind strong earthworks, and keep up a continuous fire day and night. The Reb's line is but three hundred yards from our Infantry; so you can see we are all in pretty close quarters and one does not raise his head for sharpshooters. Last Saturday afternoon, we had one of our pieces disabled

by a Reb shot, but since then there has been very little to
do by the artillery, as the sharpshooters of both parties keep
us under cover. The 22nd Mass. is close by. They have lost
very heavy since the campaign commenced. There is not a
Woburn man left in the Co., and but one non-commissioned
officer. Geo. Harrington is all right, or was yesterday. I
was glad to hear that you had sold the old farm. I think it
sold well. Take care of yourself. I have got to close as we
are to change position. There is heavy musketry firing all
along the lines. 9 o'clock P.M.

From your son,

C. M. CUTLER.

PETERSBURG, Va., Aug 9, 1864.

Dear Brother James:

It is a long while since I have heard anything from you
or from any one. I begin to think you have got to be a
silent member. I do not even know where to direct a letter,
but heard someone say you were stopping in Somerville, so
to be close to somebody. I can judge who without much
trouble. How are you making it? Pretty well, I guess, as
I do not hear anything of your having the war fever. I am
making it tip top, getting plenty of travel, promotion,
medical attendance, clothing, etc., etc. My time will ex-
pire somewhere previous to Thanksgiving. I shall hardly
know myself when I get to be a citizen again.

I am surprised to hear that Fred had enlisted. I am
glad that he is in for no longer, and that he has no harder
chance than he has. He wrote me and wanted I should
come and see him, as he was sick. Such a thing is impossible, as one can hardly get half a mile to the rear without
some general's order. I guess he is pretty homesick, having been disappointed in a soldier's life. I can draw con-
clusions from experience, but there is about as much use in
getting homesick as there is in trying to fly without wings.
My home is where I happen to be and have my shelter tent
pitched. We have not been engaged since Saturday, the
30th of July, a memorable day.

The Reb's fort went heavenward with a few Johnnies
in their shirt tails, as we caught them napping so early in
the morning. I saw the thing go up. It seemed that there
was about half an acre of ground rising some five hundred
feet up, enveloped in fire and smoke. There were two men,
a nigger and a white man, blown into our lines. The nigger
was yet alive, but the Johnnie had settled his account. The

picket firing still goes on. I have not any more to say this time. Please write soon.

It is none of my business, but have you paid for your milk route, yet? Let me know your business, and how you are situated in the world. I shall stand on my head pretty soon, if they do not give me a lead pill beforehand, as they did a tent mate of mine, J. R. Moore, of Co. F 22d Mass. He was a brother to me. I bunked two years with him in the Regiment and agreed to travel with him when we got out of this. He belonged in Illinois. He was shot on the skirmish line through the heart. He had never been away from the Regiment a day and had never got a scratch before. So ends the history of a soldier. It is rather hard, but it is but one instance in a thousand of the cases occurring every day, in the splendid charges they talk about in the papers. Write as soon as you get this.

From your brother,   C. M. CUTLER.

———

PETERSBURG, Va., Aug. 1, 1864.
Dear Bell:

I received your letter that was mailed the 11th of July, on the 27th. It was waiting some time for me at the Battery, I being at City Point as guard on some wagons we sent there. The contents somewhat surprised me, above all, that Fred had enlisted. I am glad he is not in for any longer. I received a letter from him Saturday. He was then near Arlington Heights near Washington, and was sick. He will probably be sicker before he gets out of it, but his term is not for a great while. For the last three weeks our Battery has been lying to the rear taking things easy. Last Friday night, we were ordered to the front where we went. The grand thing opened Saturday morning about daybreak. The mines that have been so long building were sprung and the Reb. forts went up. They were somewhat taken by surprise, as our Infantry took a lot of them in their shirt tails. Saturday was a lively day. Our Infantry took one line from the Rebs but could not hold it. Whether Grant accomplished what he attempted, no one knows; but I should judge he did not. We were ordered back to our old park Sunday morning. The lines still remain the same they were a month ago, the picket and artillery firing continuously.

I am not feeling first rate myself. There is scarcely anybody that does. The water is very bad around here, and the weather is so hot and sultry that it is enough to kill most anybody. Hoping this will find you all well, etc., I remain, yours affectionately,

C. M. CUTLER.

CITY POINT, Va., Sept. 23, '64.
Dear Bell:

I received your letter of the 18th this morning. I had given up writing any more until I came home, as there is so very little of importance to write about. But on getting it, I felt in duty bound to write a few lines to gratify you at home. I do not wonder that you give up the 22nd ever coming home; not any more so than the boys themselves, as we have been promised to go at three different times and all have passed. We are getting to be much dissatisfied with this, but await our time, which they say is on or before the 8th of Oct. Do not herald this to too great an extent, as we shall not be able to stand it. There are but seven of the Woburn Co. left and they are rather weather-beaten; so do not get your expectations too high. Geo. Harrington and your humble servant make two of the number.

About the young ladies you mention in your letter. Do not anticipate or wish any gathering on my account, as I'd rather be on the skirmish line in a good smart fight than be assailed by them. I wish to be as retired as possible and go my way rejoicing.

I was very sorry to hear of Aunt Myra's surprise and capture by the invaders of her territory, but never had a very magnanimous opinion of the efficiency of her grandson or of the holding out of her commissary or ordnance dept. in case of a seige. Gen. Hartwell should be relieved of his command for not bringing up his force in time. It is a very heavy loss to the country and will have something to do with the coming election. Mr. Harker shall be relieved, as I am a Lincoln man and do not tolerate his sentiments.

C. M. C.

P. S.—Tell Fred to stop in hospital and I will call and see him.

39